THE FIVE NINE TWO

THE ENTREPRENEUR'S GUIDE TO RUNNING A SUCCESSFUL LIFE AND BUSINESS

DAN HALL

ISBN: 9798846662025

BLURB

Life as an entrepreneur is no easy task. It's not something you just decide to do one day. Entrepreneurs are people with a special kind of commitment to success. They are people who constantly see challenges ahead of them and think to themselves, *heck yeah, that's something I want to try out.* And yet, with this amount of risk-taking, failure is unavoidable. It can be daunting to continuously try, try, and try again when we keep on falling down. And yet, that's what makes us thrive as entrepreneurs.

Throughout my career as an entrepreneur, I have faced my fair share of challenges. My businesses were not always successful; in fact, many of them failed. That's part of life as an entrepreneur! The key in my experience is that I *learned.* Every failure is a way for you to learn new skills, life lessons, and to change your way of living to incorporate this new knowledge. Throughout my life, this is what I learned, and now, it's your turn to learn too.

Welcome to the 592 – the model that completely revolutionized how I do business and how I organize my personal and business life. The model is simple to implement, and yet, it may completely change how you view entrepreneurship too.

Are you ready to take control over your entrepreneurial lifestyle and finally see the success you are after? Let's go.

ACKNOWLEDGEMENTS

I wish I could say I have had nothing but successes, and I have always gotten things right, but that's simply not true. Over the past 12 years in business, I have had both brilliant successes and catastrophic failures. It was those catastrophic failures that taught me more than any success could. From the failures, I changed my life and my ways, and I was able to see the real meaning of business and life. I deeply regret some choices, decisions and actions I have made in the past and have paid the price for them. From these choices, decisions, and actions, I was able to reflect and take away life changing lessons that have enabled me to be on top of my game, running several successful businesses and helping other business owners improve theirs.

Throughout my career I have always had personal support from family from day one: my mom, dad, my sister Jade, and amazing grandparents.

Later in my career, my amazing fiancé Alisha and my 3 perfect and beautiful daughters Lilly, Willow and Eliza changed my life completely and are the reason I strive to always be better and give me the strength to always get back up stronger. Without these people by my side, I am nothing. For them always being by my side, no matter the storm we are riding, I cannot thank you enough. My love for you all knows no bounds. They have all in their own way been mentors to me, each giving me their thoughts, opinions and support.

A special mention to one man known as Martin, Marty, Jocky, Hally and many more. To me, he is Dad. Thank you for your continuous support, guidance, and love. From playing devil's advocate on an idea I have to creating cash flow spreadsheets to keep us on track to just being at the end of a phone when I need him. A man that has been through so much himself but ALWAYS puts others ahead of himself, a true Father, Friend, mentor & Hero.

Then, to my mom Sarah... What a woman, she is the definition of rags to riches, a woman that's strived to always better her life for the sake of her children, a woman that always has a positive attitude, a woman that is always learning, a woman that showed my sister and I the true meaning of unconditional love and the worth in learning. To you mom, thank you, my life would be an empty place without you.

There are many people who have influenced my life for the better and they know who they are – to you I say thank you from the bottom of my heart.

To all people that have been on a journey with me in life, thank you too. We may not have seen eye to eye nor have had a good ending to our journey together, but I still say thank you. For every encounter there is a lesson learnt for both sides, I wish you every happiness and success.

"The content of your character is your choice. Day by day, what you choose, what you think and what you do is who you become."
— Heraclitus

"No man ever steps in the same river twice, for it's not the same river and he's not the same man."
— Heraclitus

CONTENTS

INTRODUCTION

Entrepreneurship is a tough challenge to take on. In fact, it's such a particular challenge to take on that many debates have taken place to discuss whether entrepreneurship should be taught in school or whether it is, in fact, something that is simply a part of a person. In other words, while some believe that everyone has the capability to be an entrepreneur if they are provided with the right tools, others believe that it is something that one has "in them" from the beginning. Take a moment to ask yourself the following: do you believe that you have what it takes to be a successful entrepreneur? To run a successful business, and to run your *life* successfully – as the two are often much more intertwined than regular 9-to-5s – you need to *want* to be entrepreneurial. What this involves is often misunderstood. Indeed, being an entrepreneur is not about getting so rich that you can buy yourself a private jet, or becoming successful overnight after you have that one "big" idea. Instead, it is a way of life that includes a lot of failure and getting back up, a focus on constantly trying new things and seeing if they will work, and a growth mindset.

This is something that I learned throughout my life. Unlike many other authors who tend to speak about the amount of success they have experienced without talking about the failure they faced – and I'm talking about the *real* failures, not the small bumps in the road – I want to share my experience with you in all its truth. Failing is simply a part of life when you run businesses, come up with new ideas and test them out on the market. There's no way around it. If you want to succeed, you need to fail a few times. Don't believe me? Let me tell you a bit more about myself, perhaps that'll show you what I mean more specifically.

I have been running my own businesses in many different sectors for over 12 years, and 80% of them have been failures. Now, that's a strong and unexpected sentence for someone writing a book on how to be successful and the best version of yourself, right? But that's the truth! No one is perfect, and from failures come lessons. Now, the 20% of success that I have experienced has been amazing success, and that's down to the life and business lessons I have learnt from my failures.

In this book, I will talk to you about what I did wrong and how it led me to find the right path to a strong and healthy business. How? By telling you exactly what to do following a model that I created as a result of these failures. My goal is to help you skip these mishaps and not make similar mistakes or wrong choices the same way I did. This book will outline the right mindset and attitude that can change your business overnight – the 592 model. Don't get me wrong – this is not a book that will teach you that you just need to keep going and trying hard with the same methods that led you to fail in the first place. Instead, it teaches you that you need to have 5 different kinds of hobbies, 9 disciplines, and 2 plans. This is what led me to truly be successful as an entrepreneur.

Being a successful entrepreneur is not just a job – it's a lifestyle. I know, how cliché of me to say this! But it's true. You cannot be successful if you see your job as something that ends after 5 PM. You cannot be a successful entrepreneur if you only see it as a part of your life – entrepreneurship is a trait that you have. It is a part of your personality. So, it de facto applies to other aspects of your life too! The way you organize your life is based on this trait – you like taking risks and doing all kinds of projects at the same time, so you go to the gym, run a business, look for a side hustle, study, and mix in your family and socialization all in the same schedule. That's comparable to an entrepreneur scheduling different business ideas and meetings to arrange funding, and so on all at once.

To be a successful entrepreneur, you need to hold a tight grip over your life. This is what this book, and more precisely the 592 model, teaches you.

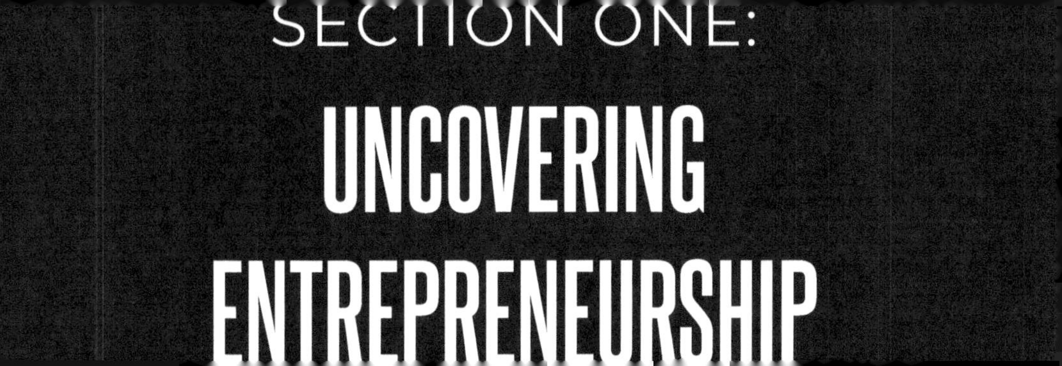

SECTION ONE:

UNCOVERING ENTREPRENEURSHIP

So, you want to be an entrepreneur – a real one. Or, perhaps you already are an entrepreneur, but you feel like you aren't fully in control of your schedule, time, projects, or might be a little lost. Maybe you also started working on your own business and do not necessarily feel like you know what it means to be an entrepreneur. To know how to create an entrepreneurial lifestyle, you need to know what exactly constitutes an entrepreneur. Well, let's look at exactly what it is.

What Is An Entrepreneur?

Jeff Bezos, Sara Blakely, Tony Robbins, Sophia Amuroso, Mark Zuckerberg, Tory Burch, Adam Neumann... all names that you most likely know very well. Perhaps you found out about them as you started being interested in entrepreneurship: you saw video on video outlining these inspiring business people and said, *yes, that's going to be me!* On the outside, it may appear as though they are successful, rich, and famous after working hard and making their way to the top. However, when you know entrepreneurship, you also know that it is much more complicated than this. Behind the success lay years of trying to sell a variety of products, different business ideas, and failed prototypes that never get approved. And yet, they *still* make it. So, what makes them different? What is it that entrepreneurs have that makes them rise to the top?

The most popular definition of an entrepreneur is someone who sets up a business, develops a new offering, cultivates customers, and seeks financing. An entrepreneur is an individual who has an idea for a new business and organizes limited resources to bring it to market. Entrepreneurship requires hard work, dedication, and a high risk tolerance. It is a noble profession, requiring years of dedication to achieve success.

Entrepreneurship is a risky endeavor, which means it requires a high level of risk aversion. Entrepreneurs manage these risks by assessing risks, deciding what level of loss they are willing to take, and teaming up with others to spread out the risks (co-founders). It's not like a blind bet; it's about defining risk aversion and avoiding it. There is a right and wrong way to become an entrepreneur, and there are specific traits that entrepreneurs tend to have that we will soon look into.

An entrepreneur is passionate about what they do. Their passion makes them great sellers. A key component of a successful entrepreneur's character is their ability to manage the business and stay focused, despite dealing with many failures. Entrepreneurs have a strong sense of personal responsibility. They don't always seek to become rich - they're often motivated by the ability to control their own destiny by choosing how they work, fund their lives, and so on.

Entrepreneurship: A Distinct Profession

People who choose entrepreneurship must be highly motivated and have a willingness to take risks. It takes a lot of work, time, and money to set up a business, and many entrepreneurs will take years before they start seeing results. Entrepreneurs must have the necessary technical skills, such as communication, productive ability, network building, active listening, or writing skills to make it big. In fact, entrepreneurship often requires one to be a jack of all trades, simply because one usually works on one's own for a long time before hiring employees becomes possible. Entrepreneurs must therefore be flexible, as they will need to learn from mistakes and try new approaches to problems – such as learning a new skill to overcome the hurdle in their way.

While most people think of entrepreneurship in terms of starting a new business, entrepreneurship can also include community-building activities and non-governmental organizations. Ultimately, entrepreneurship is more than starting a business and employing your own staff. For example, instead of focusing on making a profit, some entrepreneurs think about the value they are creating for society (social entrepreneurship). Using one's skills and talents to solve a problem is what makes this kind of entrepreneurship so important: it benefits the society as a whole.

Social entrepreneurship focuses on social problems and is growing in popularity. Many social entrepreneurs are creating products to help improve society. Social entrepreneurs are pursuing the goal of improving the world. These businesses can be nonprofit, for-profit, or hybrids of the two. Entrepreneurship is a great option for people who are tired of working for other people and struggling to find work – which is why it's often difficult to return to a 9-to-5 after working as an entrepreneur!

Common Traits Shared by Entrepreneurs

So, what makes someone an entrepreneur? There are common traits shared by entrepreneurs – many of which will be discussed in greater detail once I introduce you to the 952 model. For now, let's explore the general traits to focus on either developing further or acquiring in order to be a successful entrepreneur.

To succeed as an entrepreneur, you need to have a lot of different traits. These characteristics include a strong work ethic, the ability to adapt to change and the ability to see things from a new perspective. You should be determined and believe in your ideas, and you must have a strong belief that you will succeed. You must also be able to make decisions quickly. The ability to make quick decisions is key to your business' long-term health.

Successful entrepreneurs have high levels of alertness, a heightened sense of curiosity, and a craving for novelty. Interestingly, ADHD has been associated with a higher risk of starting a business.

This may be because people with ADHD are more likely to get bored easily with the same old routine, and thrive in times of change. Entrepreneurs often have high levels of ambiguity. Although most people perceive ambiguity as a stressful stimulus, entrepreneurs view ambiguity as an exciting stimulus that can improve performance. The ability to face rejection, disagreement, or ambiguity is also a sign that entrepreneurs have a higher level of creativity than people with low levels of this trait.

Successful entrepreneurs have a strong sense of vision. They have an idea for what they want to accomplish and they're willing to work hard to see it through. They're also adept at identifying a business' needs and leading a team to success. They're driven, have a positive attitude, and are willing to work hard to accomplish their goals. They're nonconformists by nature.

Well, does this sound like you? I thought so. While these traits are common, there are many other attributes common in most entrepreneurs – these will be covered shortly. Being an entrepreneur isn't just about having a good idea and executing it successfully. Throughout my experience as an entrepreneur, I came up with a model that includes all that it takes to see success – from your hobbies, to disciplines, and finally, the plans to have. Let's have a look.

SECTION TWO:

THE 592 MODEL

Every entrepreneur needs a solid code to live life by. After many years, I have figured out the key to this code: the 592 model. This model is simple, and yet, it has changed the way I live as an entrepreneur. It goes as follows:

You need 5 hobbies.

You need 9 disciplines.

And you need to make 2 plans.

5: Five Hobbies for a Healthy Balance

I can imagine what you are thinking – *Five hobbies?! How am I supposed to find time for five hobbies when I am already busy working non-stop to make my business work? This* is the very first step in working with this model. If you live a life in which you do not have time for five hobbies, you are not currently living an entrepreneurial life that is balanced and sustainable in the long-term. This is why five hobbies are necessary: to ensure that you instill balance in your life, and to make sure that you do not put all your eggs into one basket. Being successful as an entrepreneur is all about balance: making sure you work enough to succeed, but also taking enough time for yourself to re-boot, rest, and feel fresh to keep going. No one can work 24/7 without crashing, and burnout is the last thing we want. So, you need five hobbies – and not just any hobby of any kind.

Hobby #1: Something that makes you money

This might be the hobby that you are currently most excited about: the one that will bring in cash! It's no secret that entrepreneurs are often struggling with finding a source of finance for their business ideas. On top of that, being an entrepreneur means that you might not make an income very quickly – it can take a while until your business is profitable. To be a successful entrepreneur, you need to be as stress-free as possible. To achieve this, limiting your sources of stress is key, and being financially stable, such as by having an emergency fund and more than one source of income, is especially helpful. So, your first hobby should be something that makes money. Why not look for a side hustle?

Side hustles are a great way to supplement your income if your main source of income is not enough. You can also hone your existing skills while learning new ones. It should provide you with extra income without needing you to sit down and work for hours on end, and ideally, it would be allowing you to explore your passions. By pursuing a side hustle, you can enjoy financial security while you make money for your main project and keep most of your schedule cleared for your entrepreneurial activities.

There are plenty of ways to earn extra cash on the side. Service-oriented side hustles are often cheaper to start with and require little initial investment. They require little capital but require more expertise than a product-focused side hustle. Examples of side hustles include becoming a freelance writer, designer, spokesperson, or voice actor. You could also invest some money into a laundromat – which becomes a passive source of income – or could sell templates and software online, if you have an affinity for tech.

One great way to earn extra money on the side is by picking up seasonal gig work. You can save for your business idea by putting your paychecks towards it based on this (however, this would require you to already have a main source of income). Many side hustles are more profitable than you might think. These projects can be as simple or complex as you like.

One of the most important benefits of having a side hustle is that it can make your debt pay off faster. This can save you from paying interest over time and allow you to put a larger chunk towards paying off your debts, which increases your credit score, and which makes it easier for you to find funding later on when you have a startup or new entrepreneurial idea. Depending on the type of side hustle you choose, it might be extremely profitable! Ultimately, having additional income will increase your savings account, which can help you prepare for future expenses, or an emergency fund.

Hobby #2: Something that keeps you in shape

Your physical health is crucial if you want to be able to function as an entrepreneur. Over the past few years, we have finally come out of the hustle and grinding mindset – the era in which many entrepreneurs were told that in order to succeed, they should be working non-stop without worrying about burnout. Of course, this is not a healthy way to look at entrepreneurship. To succeed, we need to be fit, sharp, and in control. If this isn't the case, we are more prone to getting sick, which stops us and any project we are involved in right in their tracks. Genuine enjoyment of a job is the best predictor of success. So, once you reach burnout and hate what you do, your chances of success are dramatically lower. Stress can be high in today's world, so exercise is an important way to reduce it and improve your health.

Besides the many physical benefits, exercise also helps relieve burnout. It also gives you time to think, which helps you overcome unhealthy habits and gain clarity of mind. Exercise is also good for your mental health because it allows you to disconnect from the pressure of everyday life and replace it with a one-on-one conversation with yourself – you get to only focus on yourself and your own progress for that specific amount of time each day. Not only this, but it can help you manage difficult emotions as well as how you perceive yourself. Indeed, you can improve your self-esteem by exercising regularly. Feeling accomplished and in control of your body is a great way to motivate yourself and be proud of your accomplishments, and nothing is more motivating than seeing that the effort we are putting in is leading to success.

The best way to improve your overall physical health is to exercise, and the best time to do so is every day. At the very least, you should engage in 30 minutes of moderate activity five days a week. Breaking up this amount of time into two 15-minute sessions and three 10-minute sessions may help you stick to your goal of exercising for at least 30 minutes each day (going for a walk at lunch time and doing a quick home workout – there you go, all done!). However, if you find that you are unable to meet this goal, consider whether your current lifestyle fits your entrepreneurial mindset. If you don't have 30 minutes a day to solely focus on your health, you need to rethink your schedule. Your health and well-being are needed for you to succeed as an entrepreneur – make time for it!

Hobby #3: Something to stay creative

The third hobby should be something that fuels your creative side. Yes, being an entrepreneur is all about being creative, but sometimes, by solely focusing on the business aspect of creativity, we can forget about other kinds of creativity that are also important – the ones where we completely allow our minds to run freely, without having to rationalize whether an idea is possible or actionable. So, your third hobby should help you stay creative. This can be anything from writing, restoring a car, cooking, or making art.

Personal development and creativity are closely linked. Creativity is the process of blending your unique experience with outside information – and as an entrepreneur, that's what you do! However, you need to have an escape from this – you have to be able to be creative without constantly having to produce something that can turn into profit. As an entrepreneur, you are capable of tapping into your own unique perspective to find solutions to problems and innovative ideas. Now, you have to be able to do this in your personal life too. Everyone is different, so there is no one formula for achieving creativity. However, learning to tap into your own unique style and creativity can lead to success in any field.

The correlation between creativity and success is inescapable. Creative success lies in having an idea and seeing it through to completion. Creative success also involves finding your voice and continuing to grow. It is a quality that goes beyond acclaim and money. So, this hobby is not about making money, but solely about doing something that keeps your brain going and that gets you to focus on simply letting your ideas flow.

In short, creativity enhances success in all forms. By creating innovative solutions to problems, creative people create opportunities that others cannot. It also builds confidence. Confidence is important to pursue your professional goals because people who value their own uniqueness and creative ideas are more likely to have success. Whether you are an artist or into fixing cars, as a creative person, you can develop and cultivate new ideas. This is a very valuable skill to have!

The first step to fostering creativity is to learn to embrace failure. A common mistake made by creative people is avoiding failure. Failure is inevitable in life, so it's important to learn to manage it. By facing down failure and embracing your creative spirit, you'll discover what you need to do differently the next time around. This is another reason why the third hobby is about creativity: it shows you that you don't need to always succeed. You can fail, and it's okay.

The creative process is as much about creating something as it is about developing yourself. By cultivating creativity, you'll learn about yourself, and will better yourself in the process. Essentially, personal development is the process of integrating conscious learning with action, application, and growth. So, by tuning into your creativity, you are actively working on your personal development.

Hobby #4: Something to build your knowledge

The fourth hobby you take on should be something that helps you build your knowledge. It is something that helps you grow as a person by making you engage in personal development, more specifically, in continuous learning. Whether you pick up a self-help book or enroll in a course on a topic that you are passionate about, this hobby should make you feel accomplished by teaching you more. There is always something more to learn, so think of fields that you are interested in and consider how you may be able to increase your knowledge. Perhaps you can follow an online course or attend conferences on the topic. Whatever it is – make sure that it helps you learn as much as possible.

To remain relevant in today's world, you have to constantly update your skills. In the 21st century, you have to understand the multifaceted dynamics of the market. Likewise, you need to think about ways to stay highly skilled and to remain relevant in your market. This requires a continuous learning mindset and a willingness to experiment and learn.

For this reason, curiosity is a key quality that every successful entrepreneur must have, and that means taking time to have a hobby that allows you to feed this curiosity.

Entrepreneurs who have successfully launched and operated businesses have mastered self-directed learning. Oftentimes, these individuals are those who attended college but did not finish it. These individuals have shown that it is important to continue learning throughout one's lifetime. Taking courses, attending seminars, and networking with other business owners is one way to improve yourself and keep your company growing. In addition to these, self-directed learning is important for employees and entrepreneurs like you. So, think about ways that you can do this.

Learning is a lifelong adventure. To make the most of every opportunity, you need to embrace change. Changing environments is constant, so you must learn new skills to keep up with the pace. Learning is a self-motivated activity that can expand your skill set and open new doors. Continuous learning becomes a habit. It's essential for personal growth and development, and ultimately makes you a better entrepreneur.

Having more knowledge is like filling up your tank with fuel. You can learn new skills, attend training courses, and develop your ability to put your skills to use. The more you learn, the more ideas you get to become a better entrepreneur. And, as a side note – the more you know about certain topics, the easier it gets to start conversations with people! Who knows, maybe you will meet someone who could be your next investor?!

Hobby #5: Something that grows your mindset

The last hobby you should have is something that grows your mindset. So, what does that mean? Well, as an entrepreneur, you will often face situations where your mindset is tested. You will fail, even if you put in as much effort as humanly possible. You will also have situations that test your motivation and, more importantly, your dedication. This is why the fifth hobby should help you work on growing your mindset in a way that makes you more resilient to hard tasks. Consider something as simple as walking: sometimes, you will feel like going on a walk. That's great! Go for it. Other times, it might rain and you might not feel like going. However, if you choose to make it your hobby, you will still be dedicated to go because you made the decision to do so. This kind of mindset change is helpful to us as entrepreneurs: it teaches us to stick to our decisions and it pushes our dedication to its limit.

This hobby is where we can grow and develop our growth mindset. In a world where many people give up at the first hurdle, the growth mindset encourages people to push themselves beyond their comfort zones and strive for their personal best. This mindset helps people to flourish, even during difficult times. It encourages people to see failure as an opportunity to learn something new and develop, rather than a negative thing to fear. As such, your fifth hobby should be something that pushes you to develop a growth mindset.

A growth mindset requires critical thinking, letting go of perfection, and embracing learning as a lifelong process. This mindset fosters a desire to learn, grow and develop new skills and abilities. It requires an attitude that learning is fun and provides endless opportunities to improve. Ultimately, you can use this attitude to achieve greatness in life. Once you embrace the growth mindset, you will be amazed by how much more you can achieve as an entrepreneur!

Aside from this, understanding yourself is a fundamental part of personal development for entrepreneurs. A business owner must understand "why" he or she is in business – and sometimes, this is where your fifth hobby comes in. Your walk gives you time to think about what you are doing, why you are doing it, and what keeps your passion going. Success as an entrepreneur requires a clear understanding of what motivates and inspires one's actions. Understanding one's motives is a critical part of personal growth as well – and to do this, you need time to think. In a world where we are constantly surrounded by music, videos, TV shows or podcasts to avoid being stuck in silence, sometimes, the best thing to do is to force ourselves to enjoy quiet times so we *really* have to think about the rationale behind what we are doing.

Take a moment to think about the five hobbies you would like to implement. As a reminder, you should find:

1. A hobby that makes you money

2. A hobby that keeps you in shape

3. A hobby that helps you stay creative

4. A hobby that builds your knowledge

5. A hobby that grows your mindset

Once you have those in the bag, you're ready for the next step, which is working on nine key disciplines.

9: Nine Disciplines to Excel at Entrepreneurship

There are many desirable traits for entrepreneurs. Throughout my experience, I have found that the nine key disciplines you will read about in this section are the most valuable when it comes to being a successful and *balanced* entrepreneur that works on projects and ideas that work in the long-term too. Here they are:

1. Integrity
2. Commitment
3. Routine
4. Organisation
5. Goal setting
6. Networking
7. Planning
8. Risk taking
9. “Me” time

Integrity

Integrity is the practice of being truthful and showing an unwavering commitment to high moral and ethical principles. In the professional world, integrity is considered essential for effective leadership and success. Individuals with high integrity are regarded as good employees and leaders – and as entrepreneurs, they are often looked up to. They display strong moral values and consistently stick to their word. Integrity means honesty and wholeness. It means being the same person no matter what circumstances. People who act with integrity help others, are honest and trustworthy, and hence, they make great partners!

In business, integrity is essential to attract the right people, attract investors, and retain vendors. In addition to a positive reputation, integrity in business will enable a business owner to explore ideas and take the right actions to achieve success. Whether it's in your own personal life or in your professional life, demonstrating your commitment to honesty and ethics will help ensure that your business development will be successful. This is for a few different reasons, but mainly because the more integrity you have, the more people will want to work with you and will want to see you succeed. Surrounding yourself with people who trust you, value your opinion, and want to see you succeed is one of the best ways to reach success!

The path to success is not always easy. Entrepreneurs face a lot of tough decisions throughout the process that can make or break a business. Compromising your integrity for short-term gain is one of the most common mistakes entrepreneurs make. While it's tempting to make a bad decision when things aren't going as planned, integrity is a virtue you cannot buy or sell. You must never let short-term goals cloud your integrity. It might bite you in the a** later on! Trust me I know, I found this out the hard way! Stick to your convictions – it'll pay off in the longer term.

For example, consumers and companies look for authenticity in business, and as such, they'll be more likely to trust your products and services if you are known as a person with integrity. In addition, consumers are increasingly turning away from companies that compromise their integrity. This is especially true in an era where corporate social responsibility is becoming a powerful factor in consumer's buying decisions!

Commitment

Commitment is next on the list. Commitment is a verb or noun. It refers to a promise that you make to yourself to continue working hard on your goals, and it is what helps you stay on track and focused on the larger vision you have in life, even when things get tough. As an entrepreneur, you need to be committed to your business goals. Commitment is not a one-time thing, but it can be achieved through daily focus. Commitment has various advantages. First, it can encourage potential partners and investors to want to engage with your business. Second, commitment can help persuade nervous customers to adopt a new product. When they see that you are extremely committed to making their experience as your customers the best that they can imagine, they want to stay loyal.

Moreover, commitment leads to learning and growth. It is a self-fulfilling cycle that compounds exponentially. This process applies to both your personal and business life. It takes time and effort, but when you are committed to something you are passionate about, you can make a difference in your life. For example, by engaging in the 5 hobbies discussed earlier, you will have better health and your business will prosper through the soft skills you develop and the purpose that you instill in your life. By committing yourself to your goals and developing your skills, you will be more likely to succeed. Without commitment, you are setting yourself up for long-term failure. Instead, think about why you are committed to succeeding: what are you working towards? Why are you passionate about the things you do? Commitment comes easily when you have a strong sense of purpose.

Indeed, while many people are afraid of commitment, it can also bring comfort and a sense of purpose. For example, a committed artist is willing to sacrifice everything for the sake of sharing his inner vision with the world. Committed lovers put their partner's emotional well-being at the top of their priority list. Similarly, a committed performer puts his performance in the service of the audience. Commitment is an essential feature of business and it is crucial to your life as an entrepreneur because most of the time, your willingness to succeed is what will truly motivate you to work hard. Unlike other jobs, such as typical 9-to-5 jobs, you must motivate yourself. External motivation, such as needing to clock in and out, is not there. Therefore, you have to rely on your ability to commit to the goals you have set for yourself to truly see progress and success.

Routine

When we do things without having a plan or a schedule in place, it's tough to stay focused and on-track with our goals. This is especially true for entrepreneurs. As someone who works for yourself, a routine is what keeps your focus where it needs to be, and it is what ensures that you do not go off-track. You can have all kinds of routines: a morning routine, an evening routine, or even just a routine that involves you sitting down on a regular basis to evaluate the progress you have made so far. Otherwise, a daily routine can help you be as productive as possible. You can also combine your tasks with a reward for completing it. You'll be more motivated to complete the task if you have something to look forward to.

Routines can be as simple as walking every day at lunch, going to a dance class once a week, or performing a certain task that is needed to monitor your progress. Essentially, any action that is performed in a certain way regularly is a routine. The term routine can be applied to a group of actions that hold meaning to you, such as meditating in the morning to clear your head, going to the gym before work to start your day off with exercise, or spending five minutes with a gratitude journal each morning. Ultimately, your routine should help you stay in control of your productivity and should help you avoid falling into the pits of procrastination or avoidance (e.g., avoiding certain tasks because they are unpleasant to complete).

Successful entrepreneurs have routines that help them stay grounded. Starting their day with routines such as drinking water, eating breakfast, and exercising are good ways to stay focused and productive. The morning routine can be modified to include personal time, meditation, and problem-solving activities to kickstart the brain. Even better, as an entrepreneur, you should set aside time every day to dedicate to your hobbies. Creating a routine helps you balance work and life and boosts your mental health by making you feel like you have accomplished something. If you get bad news regarding a new investor, you can still look at what you accomplished throughout the day and not feel as unmotivated – it shows you that despite the bad news, there are good things happening too.

Following a routine is beneficial for a number of reasons. For one, it helps you save time as it helps you determine your schedule in advance. This allows you to prioritize your most important tasks and ensure that you have enough time for them. Because of this, routines help you achieve your goals, whether they are short-term or long-term.

Creating a routine can make you feel in control of your time and make you feel more fulfilled. By setting a routine for yourself, you'll be less likely to let yourself fall off track and get frustrated when you see a lack of results. Routines will also make you more disciplined and dedicated because they take away the need to think about what you need to do – you simply have to follow the scheduled routine you have set up.

Take a moment to think about what you would like your routine to look like. What would you include? Think about your hobbies – when will you schedule them in?

Organization

Next up, you need to be organized. The first step in becoming more organized is to acknowledge that life is messy. There will always be messes to clean up. While this is frustrating, we need to remember that life doesn't have to be a perpetual mess. Being organized doesn't mean you have to keep a picture-perfect home, or that you can never run behind on your routines and schedule. Getting organized is all about learning to manage your time well – that includes scheduling "buffer time" to catch up with any work that you may have been running behind on.

Being organized is a necessity for successful entrepreneurs. By keeping a schedule, you can avoid procrastination and stay on track. Try to set aside time each day to write down important tasks, organize your space, and set aside a day to prioritize your work. Indeed, being organized is about more than scheduling your time: it also includes organizing your finances properly, cleaning up your environment, and planning your life in an organized manner. Don't look at it from a black-or-white perspective: it isn't all work and no play. Aim for balance. Schedule time to see friends. If you have a family, schedule in time to spend with them, to clean your home, to do groceries, and so on. While being disorganized may be tempting because it requires less effort (and can seem easier to manage), it will ultimately lead to frustration and burnout. When you're disorganized, you may also make mistakes that can hurt your business because you may skip past an important detail or may dump your frustration on the wrong people or sources (e.g., your family, partner, or friends). Keeping a list of all your tasks will give you clear direction and allow you to prioritize them properly, and more importantly, scheduling them – and sticking to the schedule! – will help you avoid procrastinating on them.

Goal-Setting

Throughout this book, I mentioned the concept of goal-setting a few times. There is a reason for this: just like you set routines to stay on track, you set up goals to measure your progress. Goal-setting can give people purpose, direction, and something to shoot for. When we make goals, our actions and behaviors align. A clear intention and defined timeline will help us achieve these goals. Without a clear direction and purpose, we often succumb to the 'shiny object syndrome' - the tendency to constantly change goals and pursue newer ones. This is especially the case with entrepreneurs – we see something that we like, and if we are not focused enough, we let the previous project we were working on go and we focus on this new shiny object syndrome. Yes, some ideas will be better than others, but if we constantly see a new shiny object and let everything go all at once, we simply end up with many unfinished projects. Setting goals, in this case, can help us feel a sense of purpose within the project we are working on and it can remind us to stay focused on that first project before we give the other ones a shot.

Once you've identified a goal, you should ask yourself whether it is worthy of your time and effort. If it is, then it will be easier for you to measure your progress and determine if you've achieved it. If it does not (i.e., if you are only setting it as a goal to have a goal) you will not feel motivated to work towards it. So, be honest with yourself when you set these goals: is this really something you want to achieve? If not, you have some thinking to do.

As an aspiring (or established) entrepreneur, setting goals is important. A good goal will help you visualize your end results and evaluate your past successes and failures so you can learn from them (remember the growth mindset?). Ambitious goals will push you out of your comfort zone, but they will also help you gauge your past performance and plan for the future based on what you have learned throughout your past experiences. In short, audacious goals are the ones that will give you butterflies in your stomach and inspire you to take the leap. If a goal doesn't make you excited, it might be time to change it.

While it is essential to work hard to achieve your goals, it's important to maintain a balance between personal and professional life. Setting goals is important, but you must remember to take them one step at a time. If your goals interfere with your wellbeing, re-think them. How can you incorporate more self-care and time to yourself within your schedule?

S.M.A.R.T. goals and objectives are an excellent way to set your own objectives and goals. It is a mnemonic acronym, first proposed by George T. Doran, Arthur Miller and James Cunningham in their 1981 article. The acronym stands for specific, measurable, achievable, relevant, time-bound, and realistic. Its use in goal-setting has been widely adopted by business professionals. You will feel more motivated to reach your goals when you know you're on the right track, and since S.M.A.R.T. goals focus on creating goals that you can measure, they are the best option to stay focused. This method has worked for many people, and is a good choice for anyone looking to make goals for themselves.

Networking

As an entrepreneur, networking is an integral part of your business strategy. This method helps you establish connections with influential people in your industry, either directly or through prior networks. There are many benefits to networking as an entrepreneur, from building relationships with potential partners and investors to acquiring new clients. In this day and age, you can take advantage of social media platforms to expand your reach by commenting on industry content and engaging with your followers. Networking is an effective way to gain new contacts by reducing your time spent actively seeking them out – this can be done at conferences, events, or even just at a restaurant if you end up striking a conversation with your neighbor.

Despite its numerous benefits, networking is a challenging process for some people. For introverts, this task may feel awkward and ineffective. But don't let your introversion keep you from succeeding in networking. Treat networking as a normal task and practice until you become comfortable with it. This perspective may help: ask yourself what the worst-case-scenario is. Then, think about it this way: even if the conversation is not fruitful, at least, you will have spoken to this person and they will have learned that you exist and work in a certain field. Without this initial conversation, the person would never have even heard about you. This is like putting your foot in the door. Once you get used to it, you'll be a pro in no time, and once you will have gained confidence, you'll be able to network with ease and build your business more efficiently.

Successful entrepreneurs have a proven strategy to get more business. To network effectively, they meet successful business people, exchange ideas, and get referrals. Besides attending networking events, entrepreneurs can also contact people from their circles of friends, family, and acquaintances through email and social media. However, this strategy will be most effective when you network with people who are interested in your business – do not focus on speaking to every single person alive about your business as you will be wasting precious energy. Instead, focus your energies on meeting people who already have some kind of interest in what you are doing.

Planning

Planning has its similarities to organization, but it is different in that it focuses specifically on planning for the future. Just like your S.M.A.R.T. goals should be based on the larger vision you have for the future, you can plan your time and schedule in accordance with your vision. A plan is a set of decisions made to achieve specific objectives. It involves the selection of the purpose or objectives to be accomplished and the analysis of data (data points can be as simple as the "measurable" aspect of your S.M.A.R.T. goals: whether you have hit your social media metrics this week, or whether you reached your goal of finding a new client this month). The goals of planning are generally the improvement of the company's present or future state – in your case, it applies both to your business and your personal life as your life as an entrepreneur is intertwined with your work. A plan is also a predetermined course of action to achieve those objectives. It can be categorized by its importance, level, approach, or time period.

Naturally, planning is also necessary within your business. The planning process is a continuous process. It is necessary to take into account the lead time of the products and services, capital investment time, and expected availability of raw materials and components. Proper planning is the foundation of all management functions. Without proper planning, no management activity can be effective or efficient. Therefore, planning is not only about doing it in your personal life, but about considering every small aspect of your business when organizing its development over the coming years.

One of the best ways to ensure success as an entrepreneur is to plan early. This includes starting early asset protection and income tax planning – don't make the mistake of leaving the bookkeeping to the last minute. In addition, early planning also prepares entrepreneurs for future capital infusions. A financial plan should address short and long-term goals, as well as future growth prospects. An entrepreneur should also consider making stock investments. Planning for retirement is essential for the health and financial security of your company too, and for your own financial safety as well.

There are countless examples of people who have failed because they did not plan their steps. From failed projects to failed governance, failed exams to failed startups, this is the reason behind many failures. After all, success is not an accident; it is the result of deliberate actions taken one step at a time.

Risk-Taking

As an entrepreneur, you probably **love** risk. You see it as an opportunity to create something incredible, new, and groundbreaking, as opposed to a potential failure. This is what differentiates you from others – you **want** to take risks because the potential outcome almost always outweighs the risks.

As an entrepreneur, risk-taking is an inevitable part of your business. As a new business owner, you are likely to be risking personal finances, reputation and name, assets, and more. You may also be risking your dream of building a thriving business because you never know whether one mistake could cost you more than you can handle. But you also know that the rewards that come with risk-taking often far outweigh any potential downfalls. That being said, risk-taking should be calculated. You need to know what you are getting yourself into! Don't be impulsive – take risks, but only those that are logical and rational.

You already understand that you need to take risks to succeed. In business, you will be constantly experimenting with new ideas, technologies, and processes. The best way to stay ahead of the competition is to be an early adopter, and that involves taking the risk that the product won't make it. Nevertheless, risk-taking will give your business a competitive edge. That being said, be sure to consider your tolerance level for risk. For example, can you handle the stress that comes with it? Can you financially recover from it if it fails? As with any endeavor, you'll have to face challenges along the way, but remember that they are valuable lessons to learn from.

Lastly, as an entrepreneur, you'll need to accept that your ideas may not pan out, and that you may be wrong. But risk-taking as an entrepreneur is necessary for your business to be sustainable and grow. You need to be comfortable with the fact that your company may not work out as expected, and you'll often need to risk your own money to succeed. As you grow as an entrepreneur, you'll also need to manage your risks and learn to spread them across multiple business ventures.

The best way to take risks is to utilize your unique qualities to benefit your company. The right combination of creative thinking and strategic thinking will help you achieve success. Once you expand your business, there should also be a culture of accepting mistakes within your team, as they are necessary for success. Mistakes will expose any weaknesses in your team and may point to areas that need improvement. Risk-taking should be an ongoing process that adjusts itself to each situation – not something that you do once and never again, the second something doesn't go according to plan.

"Me Time"

And finally, you need to prioritize "me time," which is also known as self-care time, where you fully focus on your wellbeing and leave aside any discussions surrounding work, goals, or your vision. We cannot always be at the top of our game – we need time where we can just *be* without the pressures of life weighing down on our shoulders.

Self-care is the act of taking care of one's body, mind, and spirit. It can be defined as any activity that promotes health or manages illness. We all engage in some form of self-care every day. Food choices, sleep, exercise, and dental care are just a few of the many behaviors that we engage in every day. These are usually unintentional forms of self-care: we do them because they are needed to survive or because we have made a habit out of them. To establish a good balance in your life, intentional self-care should also be on your schedule.

The concept of self-care combines several different approaches, including promoting physical health and mental well-being. By engaging in regular physical activity, you boost serotonin levels in the brain, improving your mood and energy. In addition, choosing an activity that you love will make it easier for you to make time for it. This will give you added satisfaction and motivation to continue doing it, even if you are short on time. With the number of responsibilities you have, you need to have some time where you can completely let go. For you, that might be the gym – an hour per day where all you do is focus on yourself and your thoughts. Otherwise, it might be cooking or meal prepping at the beginning of the week to set yourself up for an organized and controlled week. There are other options: meditation, taking a bath, reading, doing your nails, going to the barber's for a whisky-hot towel-shave treatment, you name it.

Mental health is an essential part of maintaining a healthy life. This includes psychological, social, and emotional well-being. It affects how we act and relate with other people. It is more than just the absence of mental illness, as it is essential to our overall well-being. In addition to preventing mental illness, self-care can contribute to a healthier life where we feel like we are in control of our actions and reactions – it gives us the alone time we need to recharge and take on all the responsibilities we have.

The most important aspect of self-care is to be aware of your needs and wants. So, take a moment to ask yourself this: what do you want to do to relax? What do you enjoy doing, and what brings you happiness and stress-relief? Once you know, introduce it into your routine(s) and schedule.

2: Two Plans to Prepare for the Unexpected

While the nine disciplines and five hobbies you take on help you feel more in control of your life, there is nonetheless no way to predict the future. This is a reality that we must live with, but also one that we can prepare for. This is the last part of the model, and it involves creating two plans:

1. A plan "A" that is the best-case scenario

2. A plan "B" to deal with the unexpected

Plan A: The Best-Case Scenario

People plan their lives and businesses to the letter, and that's great! After all, throughout this book, this is exactly what I encouraged you to do. Planning is the best way to stay on track with the goals you have, and it is also a way to spot whenever you might be losing focus. So, the first plan should be the best case scenario. It should outline what you envision as being the "big goal," where your life is headed and where you want your business to be in one year, five years, and ten years from now. To do this, you also need to have two "sub plans" within this best-case scenario plan: a business plan and a personal plan.

Business Plan

A business plan is the foundation of your business, a document outlining all the information you need to know to start and grow your business. The plan should be concise and realistic, containing the names and products/services of your business and the target audience for each. This document should also identify your competition, which may not be local. The term "competition" can mean several different things, such as product or service categories, the nature of your business, or even industry segments.

The business plan forces you to analyze your competition. All companies have direct and indirect competitors. To create a competitive advantage for your business, you must clearly define your strengths and weaknesses and take steps to gain more advantages. If you want to attract investors, you will need to have a business plan that is thorough and well organized. While it may have varying formats, a typical business plan will include sections such as an executive summary, business description, location, key team members, competition, funding sources, processes and logistics, and marketing strategies, among others – the plan you create will depend on your business needs, such as whether you want to find investors or whether you are only using the plan for your own use.

Personal Plan

Then, you have your personal plan. This is where you ask yourself where you see yourself in the near future. A great way to do this is with the following exercise. When you are ready, take a moment to envision yourself in the future. Try to think as visually as possible. Imagine where you are in the world, what you are doing, who you are with, and what your days look like. Be specific. For example, are you in a forest somewhere, in a cabin with your partner, and using the millions you amassed from your life as an entrepreneur? Otherwise, do you wake up in a penthouse in New York on your own and have your personal assistant on the phone while you prepare breakfast? What do you eat for breakfast? Then, what do you do? Do you walk to work? Uber? Take your car? What car is it? Try to think about as many details as possible. The more precise you are, the better you can plan for it. Your five-year plan can then be broken down into yearly milestones and goals, which can then be broken down into monthly and weekly goals, and finally daily habits that will help you reach these.

Your personal plan should also include the less-fun aspects of being an adult and entrepreneur: the finances, commitments, savings, income sources, and so on. You should plan when you will meet with your financial advisors, your tax advisors, and how you will organize your business – indeed, it is a part of your personal life too! For example, if you trade as a sole proprietor, you will have different tax expectations than someone who trades as a Limited Liability Company. What about your savings? You should ensure to have enough to cover at least three to six months of living expenses in an emergency fund. You should also have retirement savings, and other savings for big purchases or unexpected spending (medical bills, sudden debt, etc). Speaking of debt, you will want to plan how you will re-pay your debt. Debt interest can quickly accumulate, and the best way to avoid having to pay more than necessary is simply to pay it off as quickly as possible.

Once this is done, it's time to create your Plan-B.

Plan B: When Things Don't Go According to Plan

While Plan A is fun to come up with and leaves a lot of room for creativity, Plan B needs to be more realistic and considerate of the potential failures that you might face. Here, you will also want to separate it into two plans – business and personal. Your personal plan should consider what could happen if things do not go to plan. For example, what if there is a death in the family and you need to stop for a while? What if you get sick and you cannot work anymore? What if your partner gets sick, gets promoted and needs to move elsewhere, and so on? What if your kids start growing up, take on more extracurriculars and end up needing you to drive them around more than before? These are all situations that could happen and that could drastically change your plan, schedule, and the amount of time and energy you have to dedicate to your planned life. Think about your finances as well – always look to have a backup. Invest in stocks to make sure you have some assets, or look into real estate. Increase the amount of savings you have to be able to cover larger expenses than planned for in Plan A. Consider what would happen if you needed to stop working altogether – do you have people to delegate your work to? Do you have a side hustle to turn to if money gets tight and you need to deal with inflation and its related price increases? What if your car breaks down? Or, if you bike everywhere, what if you get into an accident? This is not to give you anxiety – but rather to tell you to expect the unexpected. Trust me, you will be glad to have done so if it does indeed happen!

Then, think about your business plan. The Plan B for the business plan should of course cover what would happen if your business were to fail. Can you get more funding? Can you get covered by the state if it goes bankrupt? To this end, entering an LLC may be a better idea than a sole proprietorship. Think about all the possible outcomes, and plan for them.

CONCLUSION

This has been quite the journey! And just like that, you are ready to take on life as an entrepreneur. Choosing this life is one that will bring you multiple challenges and tests, and yet, something tells me that this is exactly why you chose it. Take what you have learned throughout this book, implement it into your life today, and start aiming high for those goals.

During my time in business, I have made many mistakes, trusted the wrong people, made stupid and hasty decisions, took too many people on their word and lost everything in a bankruptcy – all of which is the worst feeling in the world. BUT, it's the way you bounce back, it's the way you say *"no this will not define me, this will not be me, I will achieve my goals, I will get to where I want to be!"* that makes a difference. That, right there, is the entrepreneurial spirit in a nutshell.

The ability to get up every day and keep going; that's a skill and a superpower that not many have. It puts you in a group of elites, it makes you stronger than you could ever imagine.

There are a few quotes I tend to live my life by that I'd live to leave you with.

"When you focus on you, you grow. When you focus on shit, shit grows" - Dwayne Johnson

"Trying to control what is outside of your control will control you" - unknown

"Until the deal is done, the deal is not done." - Unknown

Trust your gut, if it doesn't feel right, it probably isn't. If you were wrong, you are no worse off.

Positivity breeds positivity, negativity breeds negativity

The biggest investments you can make are in yourself.

The 592 is a code I now live my life by and have a successful and happy personal and business life. With this, I wish you the very best in your adventure that is being an entrepreneur and living your life to the fullest.

www.ingramcontent.com/pod-product-compliance
Lightning Source LLC
LaVergne TN
LVHW010118170826
845678LV00012B/2477

* 9 7 9 8 8 4 6 6 6 2 0 2 5 *